Table of Contents

Preface	1
Abstract	2
Introduction	3
Research Background	3
Research Objectives	4
Research Questions	4
Research Assumptions	4
Literature Review	5
Technical Analysis	5
Indicators and Oscillators	6
Ichimoku Kinko Hyo	7
Components	8
The Tenkan Sen and Kijun Sen	8
The "Tenkan Sen"/ "Kijun Sen" Cross	10
The Chikou Span (Lagging Indicator)	10
Stretches	11-12
Bollinger Bands	13
Squeeze	13
Breakout	13
Not a standalone system	13
Stochastic relative strength index (stochastic RSI)	14
Data and Methodology	15
Research Data	15
Technical Trading Rules	15
Key Elements of Ichimoku Kinko Hyo Chart	15
Tenkan Sen	15
Kijun Sen	15
Senkou Span A	16
Senkou Span B	16
Kumo Clouds	16
Chikou Span	16
Research Methodology	16
Step-by-step procedure for ichimoku kinko hyo calculation	16
Step-by-step procedure for bollinger bands calculation	18
Step-by-step procedure for stochastic relative strength index calculation	19
Bullish logical Functions	20
Bearish Logical Functions	21
Fixed Length Trading Strategy	22
Sharma Amalgamation	22
Technical Indicator trading list	23-24
Empirical result and Discussion	25
Descriptive statistics	25-26
Data analysis	27-28
data interpretation	29
Summary and Conclusion	30
Efficient Market Hypothesis and its impact on Technical Analysis	30
Recommendations	31
Appendices	32-33
References	34

Preface

This master's thesis documents my achievements in the 3rd semester of the Master of Science studies in Investment Management at the Coventry University. It was carried out at the School of Economics, Finance and Accounting EFA in the Faculty of Business and Law (FBL) of Coventry University.

I would like to thank my supervisor Dr. Timothy Rodgers for valuable advice and comments during the process. Furthermore, I would like to thank Dr. Jacek Nicklewski, Dr. Mohammed Newaz, Dr. George Huelene, Dr. Jin Suk Park, for insightful information about stock market trading and tips concerning technical analysis patterns.

I would additionally extend a special thank you to Kiana Danial the CEO and Founder of Invest Diva. Kiana has been an absolute inspiration and a mentor in the expertise on Ichimoku Kinko Hyo and other technical analysis techniques.

Lastly, I would also my peers Ben Kent, Shoaib Anwar and Ala'a Elganbur deserve a thank-you for being cheerful company during demo trading lab sessions, coffee breaks, as do all friends and family that have supported me throughout the implementation and writing process.

Coventry University, 2018

Tanmaya Sharma
MSc. Investment Management

Abstract

In this paper, we will study the significance of technical analysis and its impact in predicting stock price movements to generate alpha. We will study four markets, United Kingdom, United States of America, Republic of India and Canada for the purpose of this research simplicity we will use their main stock indices namely FTSE 100, S&P 500, Nifty 50 and S&P/TSX 60 respectively.

We will briefly scrutinize each technical analysis technique of Ichimoku Kinko Hyo, Bollinger Bands, and Stochastic Relative Strength Index.

We will use an amalgamation of Ichimoku Kinki Hyo, Bollinger Bands, and Relative strength to screen these stocks, we will refer to this as "Sharma Amalgamation". We will also briefly explain the inherent underlying behavioral science biases that may cause our findings to get distorted or extrapolated. Thus, we will circumvent this problem by using an inverted loss aversion theory.

Our findings evidence that technical analysis and especially "Sharma Amalgamation" can indeed be successfully used to predict stock price movements. Thereby, creating alpha (excess returns).

1. RESEARCH BACKGROUND

This research will undertake an in-depth analysis into the applied scientific workings to pondering upon the dilemma of whether technical analysis could ever be successfully used as a trading formula using a specific amalgamation of technical analysis techniques to create alpha.

This research is purely driven by the enhancement objective of profitability efficiency of an Amalgamate stock screening mechanism consisting of 3 Technical Analysis techniques: (1) Ichimoku Kinko Hyo, (2) Bollinger Bands and (3) Stochastic Relative Strength Index

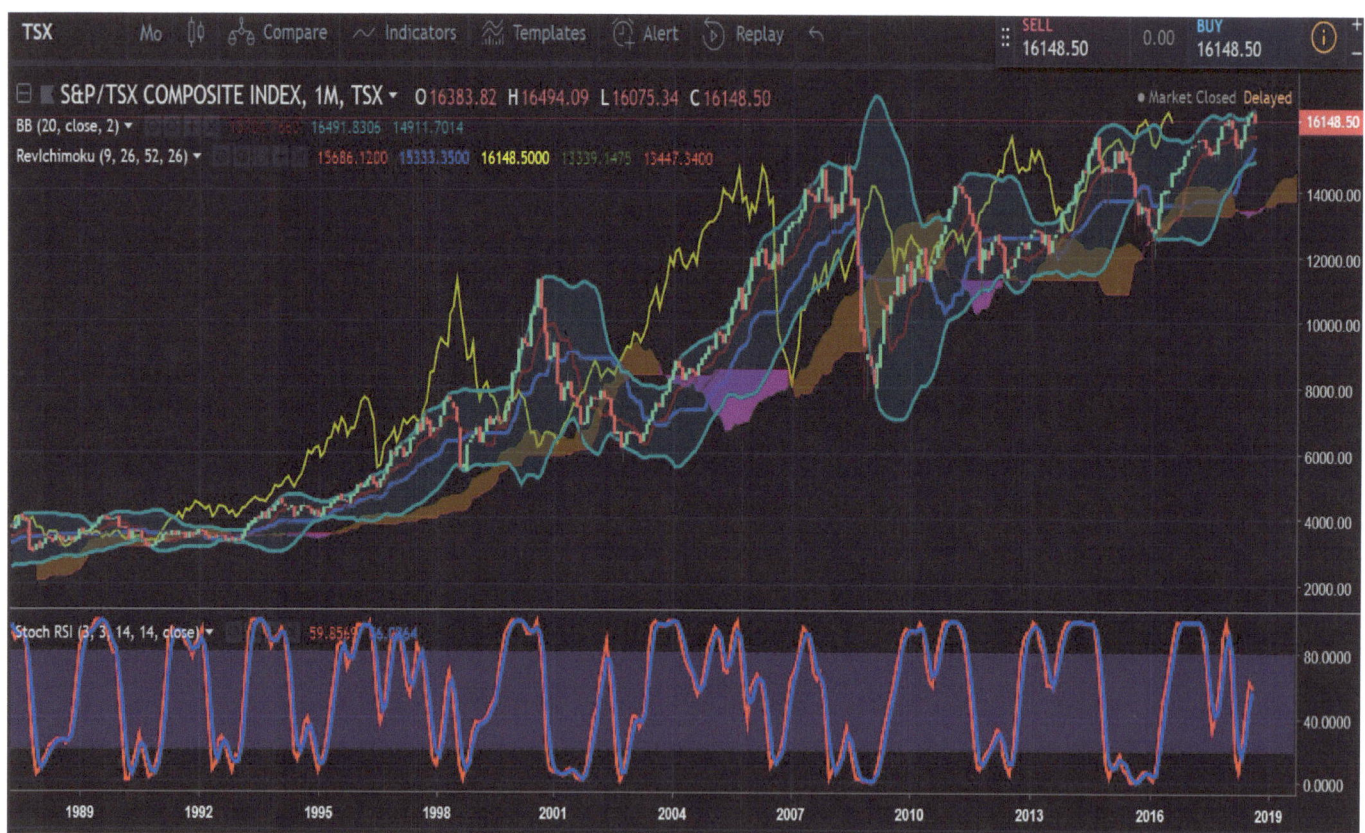

Chart 1: A chart Illustrating an amalgamated stock screening mechanism consisting of Ichimoku Kinko Hyo, Bollinger Bands and Stochastic RSI on S&P/TSX from 1989 to 2018 (Source: Tradingview)

In order to eliminate the underlying inherent behavioral biases, it is imperative to consider two economic recessions to map the profitability of our assumption. Ipso facto, a time frame from 1990 to 2018 is chosen. This timeframe inculcates two major periods of markets loss of confidence which occurred as the "Dot-com bubble" In the early 2000's and the "Subprime Housing Bubble" of 2007-09.

The research does not discount that minor regional bubbles such as the Greek crisis, the taper tantrum and the Chinese debt bubble of 2015 also occurred during these periods. However, these bubbles were contained and as a result, the markets did not face such a widespread system systemic markets loss of confidence as it occurred in the dotcom bubble and subprime housing crisis.

2. RESEARCH OBJECTIVES

The purpose of this research is to determine whether technical analysis could be successfully used to predict stock price movements. Ipso facto, by extension benefit from the second derivative of the predicting stock price movements by creating profit, which is the entire premise of investing.

3. RESEARCH QUESTIONS

In this research we specifically ask:
a. Can we trade based on buy/sell signals, oversold/overbought signals, permutations and combinations generated by technical analysis to create alpha in the United Kingdom using FTSE 100?
b. Can we trade based on buy/sell signals, oversold/overbought signals, permutations and combinations generated by technical analysis to create alpha in the United States of America using S&P 500?
c. Can we trade based on buy/sell signals, oversold/overbought signals, permutations and combinations generated by technical analysis to create alpha in the Republic of India using Nifty 50?
d. Can we trade based on buy/sell signals, oversold/overbought signals, permutations and combinations generated by technical analysis to create alpha in Canada using S&P/TSX 60?

4. RESEARCH ASSUMPTIONS

This is one of the most important section of our dissertation if "Research Question" was the bedrock of our research then, ipso facto "Research Assumptions" is the blueprint based on which our research will mature into advanced stages of determining whether based on our assumptions we could create alpha or indeed we are researching mundane chaos.

Our key assumption in this research is to do we execution covenants and will enforce an embargo on short selling. According to Brock (Brock et al 1992), The results generally show that returns during buy periods are larger than returns during sell periods. Moreover, returns during buy periods are less volatile than returns during sell periods Thus, pursuant to these conditions we would go long when our indicators are indicating a buy signal and oversold or (the first one) on an amalgamation on our stock screening mechanism, and we will hold the position and exit only when we see buy signal with the overbought signal (the first one). However, at this point ipso facto we will not re-enter into a short position as this is indicated by our "Research Assumption" from the underlying reasoning (Brock et. al 1992) in this section due to a self-imposed embargo on short selling for the purposes of research and an inherent underlying risk aversion.

This covenant is primarily driven by two reasons first reason is that losses are potentially unlimited in an out of the money short position. Secondly, it is an inherently underlying phenomenon of Behavioural Finance. Many of us are very well versed with the phenomenon called loss aversion in behavioral finance where investors sell their winning positions, but they hold on to their losing positions in hope of a recovery over a longer time horizon.

However, in trading the loss averse investors are plagued with disposition effect and loss tolerance, so under an Efficient Market Hypothesis system often once the price falls too rapidly and too quickly. An already rapidly declining market is flooded with irrational exuberance caused due to a plethora of sell orders until bargain hunters re-enter the market to provide relief. This goes against prudent investment management theory and empirical evidence and thus we will not enter into a short position.

The researcher niches onto "Sharma Amalgamation" a stock screening mechanism, the notion of this research paper being that "Sharma Amalgamation" is a mechanism of combining buy and oversold signals with Sell and overbought signals. A combination of these two kinds of technical analysis is similar to the symbiosis as evidenced in science. symbiosis in science is any type of close and long-term biological interaction between two different type of biological organisms. In symbiosis, both parties stand to benefit from mutual cooperation as opposed to what they could achieve individually.

Similarly, buy and sell signals omit the overall trend of the underlying, whereas overbought and oversold signals omit the ability to time entry and exit into the underlying. Sharma Amalgamation capitalizes on this perfect pairing to confirm the execution decision in light of timing the entry or exit and confirmation of overall trend of the underlying.

TECHNICAL ANALYSIS

Technical Analysis is an analysis technique based on examining the charts of an underlying by scrutinizing the past and current demand and supply forces presented in various formats, the most common is candlestick patter.

A chart consisting of the only candlestick is referred to as a "Naked price action chart". Once indicators are added on top of a naked price action chart analysis can be performed in a complex manner. The simplest way of performing the analysis is looking at the candlesticks patterns such as "Hammer" or "Inverted Hammer" which help in forecasting future demand and supply trends.

This can further be enhanced by adding mezzanine tranche first derivative technical indicators such as simple moving averages or exponential moving averages or oven MACD. An increase of Second derivative technical indicator will provide finer results, indicators such as Ichimoku Kinko Hyo which is the second derivative of MACD and Stochastic Relative Strength Index which is the second derivative of Relative strength index can be used.

Charles Dow is the founding father of technical analysis given his views on Dow theory which served as the back bone for technical analysis arguments.

Brock et al (1992) Brock et al argue that Technical Analysts attempt to forecast prices by the study of past prices and a few others related summary statistics about security trading. They believe that shifts in supply and demand can be detected in charts of market action. Brock et al further educate us that technical analysis is considered by many to be the original form of investment analysis, dating back to the 1800s.

This is imperative as we will further notice the implications of Ichimoku Kinko Hyo which was not developed until the mid-1900s by a journalist called Goichi Hosoda in Japan.

However, the Technical analysis is not the preferred mode of many old-school analysts. One of the critics of technical analysis Malkiel (1981) discusses the attitude of academics towards technical analysis:

> *"Obviously, I am biased against the chartist. This is not only a personal predilection but a professional one as well. Technical analysis is anathema to the academic world. We love to pick on it. Our bullying tactics are prompted by two considerations: (1) The method is patently false; and (2) its easy pick on. And whilst it may seem a bit unfair to pick on such a sorry target, just remember: it is your money we are trying to save"*

Brock et. al (1992) argues *"all major brokerage firms publish technical commentary on the market and individual securities, and many of the newsletters published by the various "experts" are based on technical analysis"*.

Brock et.al (1992) importantly argues that two reasons enlighten the existence of predictability variation in stock returns have been recommended:

1. Market inefficiency during which prices deviate from the fundamental values
2. Markets are efficient, and the predictable variation can be explained by time-varying equilibrium returns

Brock et al (1992) also argue that "there is no evidence do far that unambiguously distinguishes these two competing hypothesis.

Indicators and Oscillators

(Kuepper N.d.) Firstly, Kuepper argues that there are primarily two types of technical indicators (1) leading Indicators and (2) lagging Indicators.

Leading indicators try to front run price movements and try to predict the future. These indicators are at the epitome of their efficiency through periods of sideways or non-trending price movements since these indicators can help identify breakouts or breakdowns.

Lagging indicators tail price movements and act as an evidencing tool. These indicators are more efficient whilst trending periods where they can be used to confirm that a trend is still robust or if it is tapering out.

(Kuepper N.d.) Secondly, Kuepper further educates us that Indicators can additionally be disintegrated into two broad categories based on how they source themselves to their existence (1) Oscillator and (2) Non-Bounded

Oscillators are the most familiar type of technical indicator and are predominantly bound within a range. For example, an oscillator may have a low of 0 and a high of 100 On one hand, zero in such a scenario indicates an oversold situation, whereas, on the other hand, 100 represents overbought conditions. An Example of this kind of indicator is the Stochastic Relative Strength Index, which is used as one of the indicators in this research.

Non-bounded indicators are scarcer, however, they still help to form buy and sell signals as well as show strength or weakness in these trends. However, these indicators engineer this in many ways without the use of a set range.

(Kuepper N.d.) Thirdly, Kuepper insists that Indicators create buy and sell signals by (1) crossovers or (2) divergence.

Crossovers are the most admired technique whereby the price moves through a moving average or when two moving averages crossover. An example of this is the Tenkan Sen and Kijun Sen from Ichimoku Kinko Hyo.

Whereas, **Divergence** occurs when the direction of a price trend and the direction of an indicator are moving in opposite directions, which tends to suggest that the direction of the price trend is weakening.

(Kuepper N.d.) Finally, Kuepper asserts that Indicators can be extremely useful in momentum recognition, trends, volatility, and other aspects of a security. However, it's imperative to note that indicators work to the efficiency epitome when amalgamated with other forms of technical analysis to maximize the probability of success.

Ichimoku Kinko Hyo

A chart Illustrating Ichimoku Kinko Hyo on Nifty 50 from 2002 to 2015 (Source: Tradingview)

(Muller 2013) Muller argues that the "Ichimoku Kinko Hyo" (or equilibrium at a glance) charting system offers deep insight into market dynamics in any timeframe analysis, from "High-frequency trading" to a "Grand Super-Cycle" Investment Guide (Though it is mainly used in the daily, weekly & monthly candle perspective).

Ichimoku Kinko Hyo often referred to as Ichimoku or Ichimoku Clouds is a technical analysis process which advances on the naked price action candlestick charting to improve the efficiency of projected price movements.

This technique was developed in the late 1930s by Goichi Hosoda, a Japanese journalist who used to be known as Ichimoku Sanjin, which translates as "What a man in the mountain sees". He spent thirty years perfecting the technique before releasing his findings to the general public in the late 1960s.

Ichimoku Kinko Hyo translates to **'one glance equilibrium chart'** or **'instant look at the balance chart'** and is seldom referred to as **'one glance cloud chart'** based on the unique 'clouds' that feature in Ichimoku charting.

(Muller 2013) However, what is a most imperative revelation as educated by Muller is the fact that this system consists of several parts all of which can be singled out as standalone tools of technical analysis. Muller further elaborates that these standalone fragments of indicators offer partial insights regarding trends and support/resistance and advice entry/exit strategies.

The Ichimoku Clouds are also referred to as Kumo clouds. Ichimoku is a moving average-based trend identification system and because it contains more data points than standard candlestick charts, provides a clearer picture of potential price action.[3] The main difference between how moving averages are plotted in Ichimoku as opposed to other methods is that Ichimoku lines are constructed using the 50% point of the highs and lows as opposed to the candle's closing price.

Ichimoku factors time in as an additional element along with the price action, similar to William Delbert Gann's trading ideas. Popular in Japan, Ichimoku is gaining traction in the west through proponents of its charting accuracy such as Lincoln FX and Ichi360.

COMPONENTS

Muller (2013) argues that all components are primarily moving averages which have been tweaked in different ways and programmed to move higher or lower with the underlying currents that ultimately (and hopefully) create trends.

Muller (2013) settles the notion that they are constructed to capture shorter and longer oscillations within trends to indicate the direction of the trend(s), to generate buy & sell signals, to identify "stretches"(where the market is thought to be "overbought" or "oversold") and to provide the trader with potential levels of support and resistance (now and in the future).

THE TENKAN SEN AND KIJUN SEN

Illustration 1.1.1 (Source: Muller 2013)

Muller (2013) Muller confirms the notion that Kijun sen depicts the actual support. He further elaborates that this way the average also goes flat when there are no new higher high and/ or lower low during the measured period that changes the calculation result it also displays better non-trending conditions through a flat equilibrium point rather than a sloping average. This is shown in illustration 1.1.1

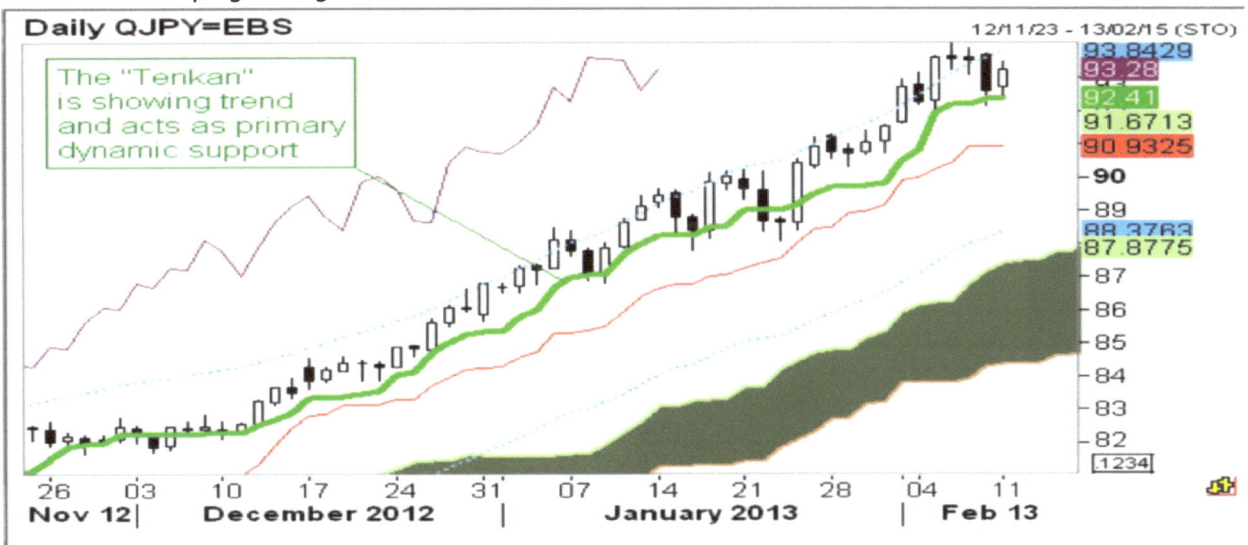

Illustration 1.1.2 (Source: Muller 2013)

Muller (2013) Muller educates us when "Tenkan Sen has positively sloped the short term oscillations within a broader perspective are thought to favour the upside and when spot trades above the "Tenkan" its thought to act as the first near-term support level. The opposite rules when it is negatively sloped."

Muller (2013) Muller further argues that "breaking a bullishly sloped "Tenkan" from above is normally not enough to justify a short position since it is merely a warning that the underlying impulse may reverse into a correction"

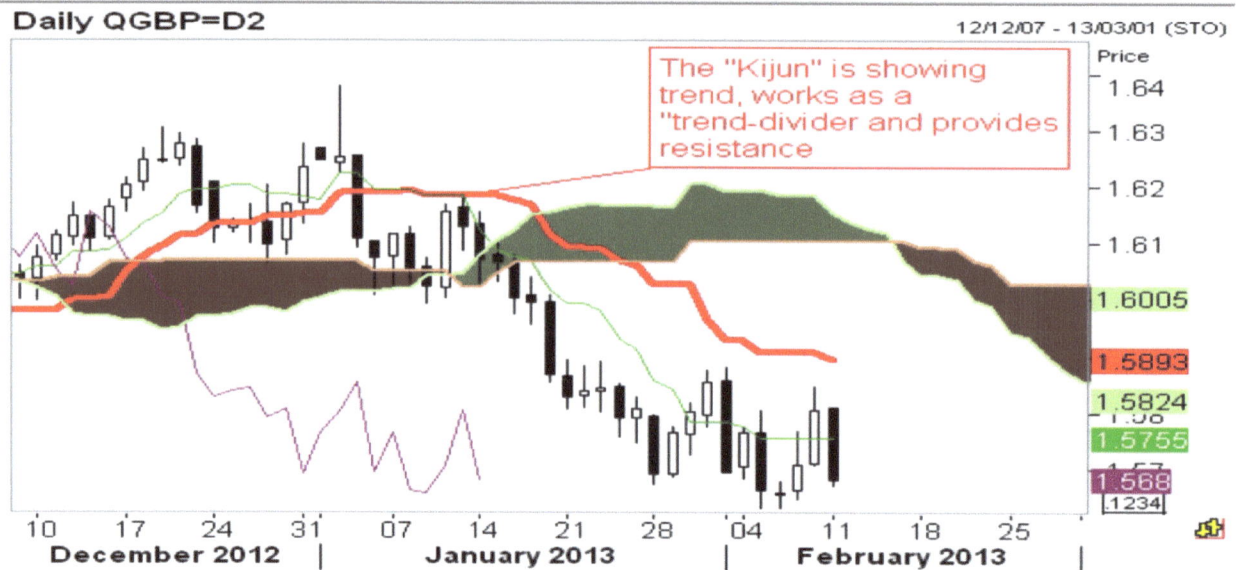

Illustration 1.1.3 (Source: Muller 2013)

Muller (2013) confirms the notion that the "Kijun Sen" is slower and normally thought to better show "Equilibrium" and thus the trend in the timeframe analysed. Kijun Sen can also be said to be the "trend-divider", so when trading above it, the market is crudely thought to be trending higher, and when trading below it, the market is considered to be trending lower.

Muller (2013) also objectively asserts that however, the slope (if any) of the "Kijun Sen" is also essential to determine where the undercurrent is flowing and if it is doing a good job doing so. A flat "Kijun" indicates short-term consolidation and quite often such conditions attract a market that has run slightly ahead of itself. Once a short-term correction is completed, closer to the "Kijun" the underlying move may continue in line with the overall trend in the market and timeframe analyzed.

THE "TENKAN SEN"/" KIJUN SEN" CROSS

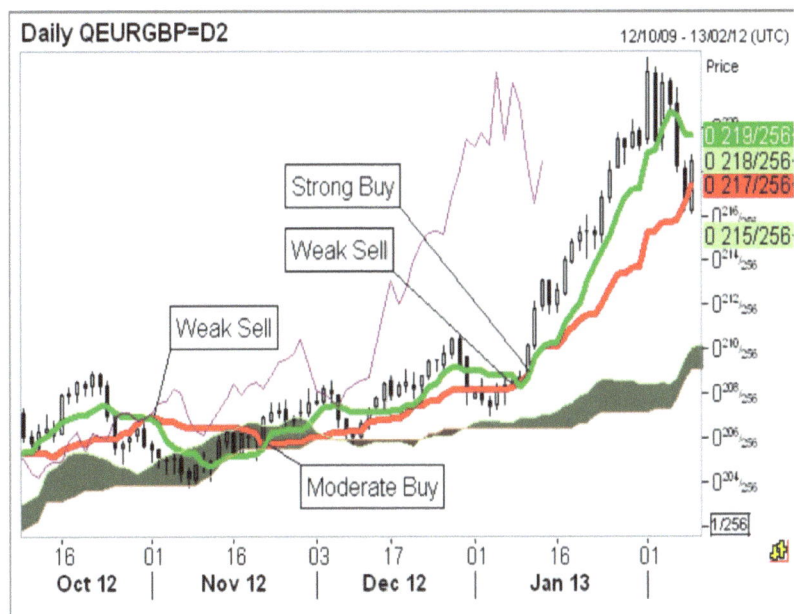

Muller (2013) then educates us that "the faster Tenkan Sen and the slower Kijun Sen conduct repeated crossovers. These shifts are considered as buy or sell signals, depending on whether the Tenkan Sen crosses the Kijun Sen from below (Buy signal) or if it crosses from above (Sell signal). A bullish signal below a positively sloped "cloud" is a buy signal, but considered weaker, a bullish crossover inside the "cloud" (preferably when it's bullishly slanted) is defined as moderate and a bullish crossover above a positively sloped "cloud" is considered strong. The opposite obviously rules in the case of a bearish crossover (over the "Kumo" or "Cloud" = weak, inside the "Kumo" moderate and below it = strong)"

THE CHIKOU SPAN (LAGGING SPAN)

Muller (2013) argues that "The "Chikou Span" or "Lagging Span" is exactly what its name depicts. It is simply today's spot shifted 21 periods backward (the original setting is 26 periods). This line is used to compare today's price with the price 21 periods back. A current spot above the spot 21 periods back implies uptrend and a current spot below the spot 21 periods back indicates downtrend"

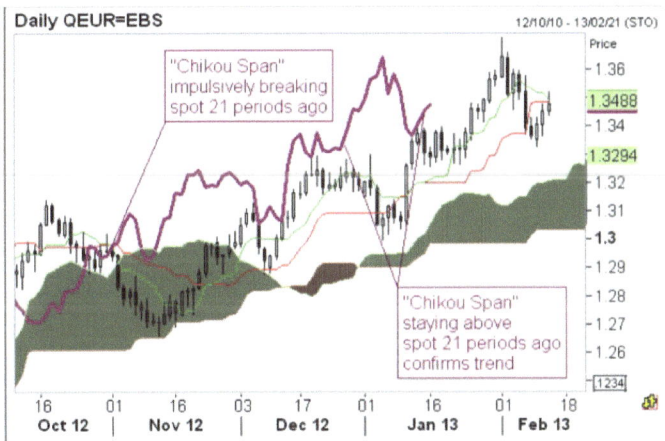

Muller (2013) argues "A bullish "Chikou span" cross through spot 21 periods ago occurs above the "Kumo" is thought to be a stronger signal than if the cross appears in or below the "Kumo" and the opposite obviously rules for a bearish cross: stronger below the "Kumo" than if it materializes in or above it."

Muller (2013) argues that "Another practical tool is to draw a horizontal support and resistance levels based on "Chikou span" since it is recorded through important closing prices (perhaps less valuable in 24hr markets like FX, while in equities and bonds the closing price is a more important piece of information)."

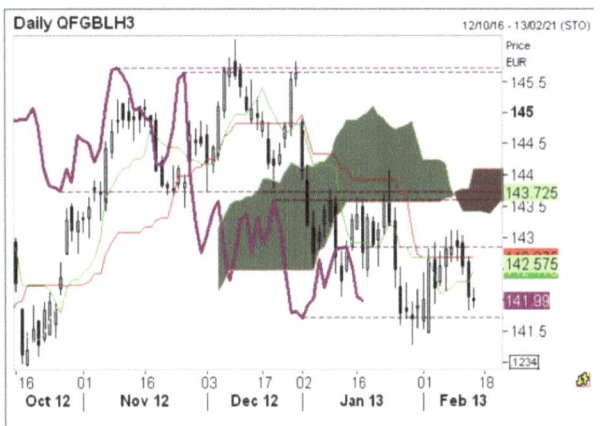

STRETCHES

Muller (2013) argues that "any trend is essentially an oscillating process around a fair value. In a trend, this fair value or "equilibrium" change over time" as indicated in illustration 1.1.5. below. Muller (2013) further argues that "this is true for whatever timeframe is analyzed. Within any timeframe, there are different reasons for participation which may be shorter or longer term oriented".

Muller (2013) also argues that Ichimoku Kinko Hyo can be used for medium-term or weekly candle time frame or long term- monthly candle horizon or other time frames ranging from "Grand-Super cycle" or even "Tic-by-tic".

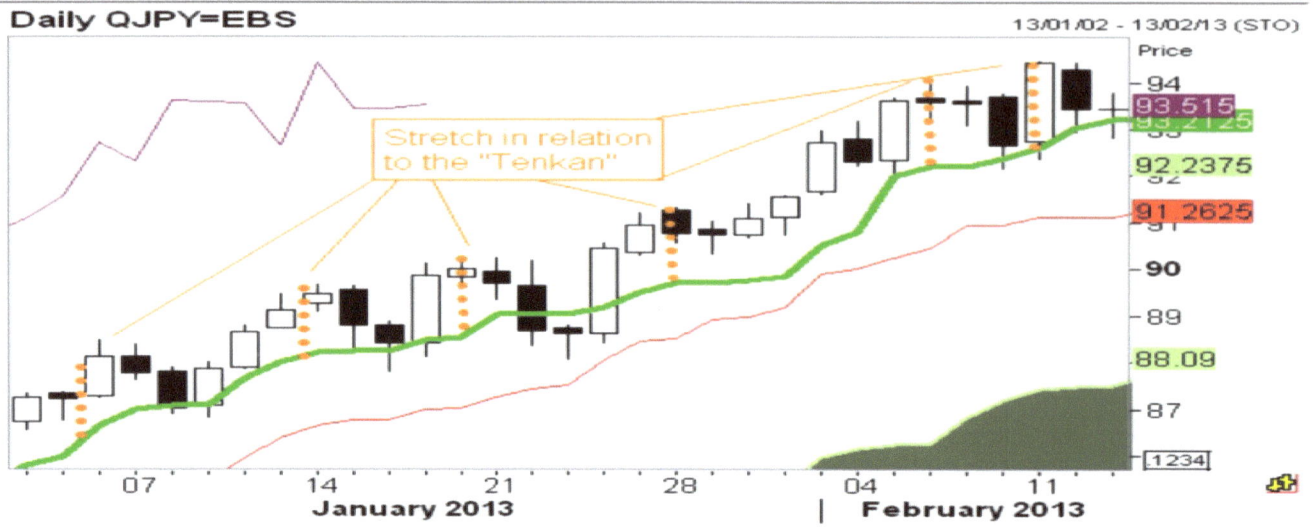

Illustration 1.1.5 (Source: Muller 2013)

Muller (2013 further argues that "A stretch may be defined through the sheer distance between spot and the fair value or "equilibrium" of choice. If overall uptrend indications are in place and spot is considered as stretched compare to selected measure of "equilibrium" after a correction lower has taken place, a long position should be considered and if the impulse reaches a wide distance to "equilibrium" on the other side and in line with the trend, large enough to make trend following positions likely to be less additionally rewarding, take-profit or at least reduction should be considered. The opposite obviously rules for conditions in a downtrend"

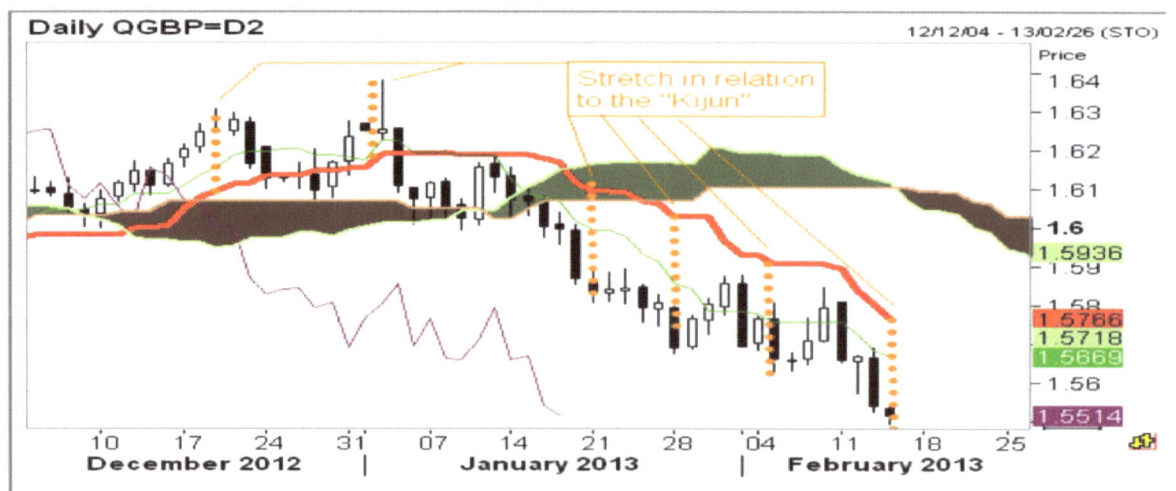

Illustration 1.1.5 (Source: Muller 2013)

Illustration 1.1.5 (Source: Muller 2013)

Muller (2013) also argues that "another angle may be plausible, if the market is trending strongly, the stretch as measured by the distance to "fair value", may be calculated with the slower "Kijun" in mind, while the stretch during the correction could refer to the distance to the "Tenkan" instead"

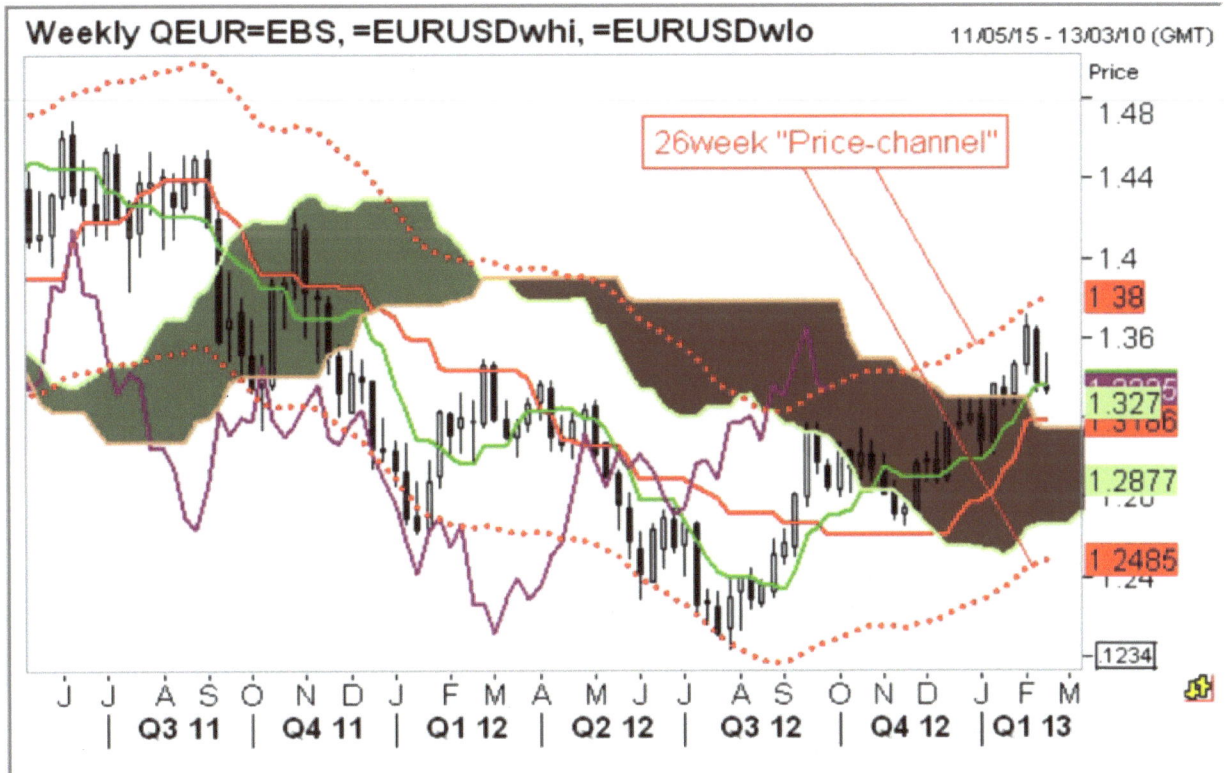

Illustration 1.1.5 (Source: Muller 2013)

Bollinger Bands

A chart Illustrating Bollinger Bands on FTSE 100 from 1989 to 2018 (Source: Tradingview)

Bollinger Band was developed by famous technical trader John Bollinger. This technical analysis tool is plotted two standard deviations away from a simple moving average.

Bollinger Bands are a highly popular technical analysis technique because it helps to measure the market. This measure aid helps many traders identify a good entry/exit strategy. This entry/exit is derived from the belief the closer the prices move to the upper band, the more overbought the market, and the closer the prices move to the lower band, the more oversold the market. John Bollinger has a set of 22 rules to follow when using the bands as a trading system.

The Squeeze

The squeeze is the central concept of Bollinger Bands. When the bands come close together, constricting the moving average, it is called a squeeze. A squeeze signals a period of low volatility and is considered by traders to be a potential sign of future increased volatility and possible trading opportunities. Conversely, the wider apart the bands move, the more likely the chance of a decrease in volatility and the greater the possibility of exiting a trade. However, these conditions are not trading signals. The bands give no indication when the change may take place or which direction price could move.

Breakouts

Approximately 90% of price action occurs between the two bands. Any breakout above or below the bands is a major event. The breakout is not a trading signal. The mistake most people make is believing that that price hitting or exceeding one of the bands is a signal to buy or sell. Breakouts provide no clue as to the direction and extent of future price movement.

Not a Standalone System

Bollinger Bands are not a standalone trading system. They are simply one indicator designed to provide traders with information regarding price volatility. John Bollinger suggests using them with two or three other non-correlated indicators that provide more direct market signals. He believes it is crucial to use indicators based on different types of data. Some of his favored technical techniques are moving average divergence/convergence (MACD), on-balance volume and relative strength index (RSI).

The bottom line is that Bollinger Bands are designed to discover opportunities that give investors a higher probability of success.

Stochastic Relative Strength Index (Stochastic RSI)

A chart Illustrating Bollinger Stochastic RSI on S&P500 from 1981 to 2018 (Source: Tradingview)

(Investopedia N.d.) Investopedia educates us that the Stochastic Relative Strength Index is an indicator used in the technical analysis under this indicator we evidence ranges between zero and one hundred and is generated by utilizing the Stochastic Oscillator method to a set of Relative Strength Index (RSI) values rather than standard price data. (Kuepper N.d.) As argued by Kuepper, we learn that the Stochastic Relative Strength Index is an Oscillator as discussed in the Technical Analysis Chapter.

(Investopedia n.d.) Investopedia educates us that using RSI values inside the Stochastic formula permits traders an idea of whether the current RSI value is overbought or oversold - a measure that becomes predominantly useful when the RSI value is restricted between its signal levels of 20 and 80.

(Investopedia n.d.) Investopedia educates us that the Stochastic Relative Strength Index was developed by Tushar Chande and Stanley Kroll and detailed in the book The New Technical Trader published in 1994.

(Investopedia n.d.) Investopedia further argues that while technical indicators already existed to show overbought and oversold levels, the two developed Stochastic Relative Strength Index to improve sensitivity and generate a greater number of signals than traditional indicators.

(Investopedia n.d.) Investopedia preaches to us that the Stochastic Relative Strength Index is calculated using the following formula:

$$\text{Stochastic Relative Strength Index} = \frac{(RSI - Lowest\ Low\ RSI)}{(Highest\ High\ RSI - Lowest\ Low\ RSI)}$$

1. RESEARCH DATA

This is a neologistical concept in nascency and with every such case, it follows the principles of Schrodinger's cat which is an anecdote stating that the concept is perceived both existent and non-existent ipso facto until tested through mechanisms.

The raw data dump series sequences used in this study is the Standards and Poor 500 (S&P 500), Finance Times-Stock Exchange 100 Index (FTSE 100), National Stock Exchange 50 (Nifty 50 or CNX Nifty) and Standards and Poor/Toronto Stock Exchange 60 (S&P/TSX 60). Thus to pursue the research we used daily share price information from 01 January 1990 to 15 June 2018 for S&P 500, FTSE 100, Nifty 50 and S&P/TSX 60 (For certain indices the data is not available from 01 January 2018 the next earliest available data has been used) – a collection of 30 Years of daily data.

To download this data, we have used Bloomberg L.P. for education as Coventry University has an educational Bloomberg L.P. access.

The stocks included in these indices have seldom changed for developed markets whereas the occurrence is more common for countries like India and Canada. Ipso facto, changes in S&P 500 and FTSE 100 in its nascency were more common. Since inception, across the board, the indices have included market leaders, well-known and actively traded stocks, and while concerns about synchronous trading may not be incorrect on a macro level amongst comparable economies, intra country stocks trading does position itself as less of a concern on a nonsynchronous trading level. A prime instance of this is the fact that India and USA often operate in coetaneous tandem with each other with positive correlation as both of them are major oil consumers. Whereas Canada is a major oil producer and operates in an inverse proportion to oil consumers.

Technical Trading Rules

Three of the most unique and widely utilized technical rules are investigated: Ichimoku Kinko Hyo (which indicates buy or sell signals), Stochastic Relative Strength Index (which indicates Overbought or Oversold signals) and lastly, Bollinger Bands (which indicates Overbought or Oversold signals).

According to

Key elements of the Ichimoku Kinko Hyo chart

TENKAN-SEN

Calculation:

$$\left\{\frac{highest\ high\ +\ lowest\ low}{2}\right\}$$

Tenkan Sen is calculated for the last 9 periods. Tenkan Sen is primarily used as a signal line and a minor support/resistance line.

KIJUN-SEN

Calculation:

$$\left\{\frac{Highest\ High\ +\ Lowest\ Low}{2}\right\}$$

for the past 26 periods.

This is a confirmation line, a support/resistance line, and can be used as a trailing stop line.

SENKOU SPAN A
Calculation:

$$\left\{\frac{Tenkan\ Sen + Kijun\ Sen}{2}\right\}$$

This is plotted 26 periods ahead. Also called leading span 1, this line forms one edge of the kumo or cloud

SENKOU SPAN B
Calculation:

$$\left\{\frac{Highest\ High\ +\ Lowest\ Low}{2}\right\}$$

Senkou span B is calculated over the past 52 time periods and plotted 26 periods ahead. Also called leading span 2, this line forms the other edge of the kumo.

KUMO CLOUDS
Kumo clouds are the space between Senkou Span A and Senkou Span B. The cloud edges identify current and potential future support and resistance points.

CHIKOU SPAN
Chikou span calculation: today's closing price projected back 26 days on the chart.

Also called the lagging span it is used as a support/resistance aid.

2. **RESEARCH METHODOLOGY**

Research Methodology is a complex multivariate successive procedure which involves a keen eye for detail.

Step-by-step Procedure for Ichimoku Kinko Hyo calculation:
Step 1:

We begin by calculating the <u>highest high for the 9 periods</u>.

For this, we use the excel formula

$$= max\ (High\ of\ period\ 1:high\ of\ period\ 9)$$

The data for a high of the respective period was respectively downloaded via Bloomberg L.P. for Education

Step 2:

We begin by calculating the <u>Lowest low for the 9 periods</u>.

For this, we use the excel formula

$$= min\ (Low\ of\ period\ 1:Low\ of\ period\ 9)$$

The data for low of the respective period was respectively downloaded via Bloomberg L.P. for Education

Step 3:

We now calculate <u>Tenkan Sen (also referred to as the conversion line)</u>

For this, we use the excel formula

$$= \frac{(\text{Highest High for the 9 periods} + \text{Lowest Low for the 9 periods})}{2}$$

Step 4:

We begin by calculating the <u>highest high for the 26 periods</u>.

For this, we use the excel formula

$$= \max(\text{High of period 1}:\text{high of period 26})$$

The data for a high of the respective period was respectively downloaded via Bloomberg L.P. for Education

Step 5:

We begin by calculating the <u>Lowest low for the 26 periods</u>.

For this, we use the excel formula

$$= \min(\text{Low of period 1}:\text{Low of period 26})$$

The data for low of the respective period was respectively downloaded via Bloomberg L.P. for Education

Step 6:

We now calculate <u>Kijun Sen (also referred to as the Base line)</u>

For this, we use the excel formula

$$= \frac{(\text{Highest High for the 26 periods} + \text{Lowest Low for the 26 periods})}{2}$$

Step 7:

We will now calculate <u>Chikou Span</u>

For this, we use the excel formula

$$= \text{close index price for the period } t \text{ plotted } t - 26 \text{ behind}$$

Step 8:

We will now calculate <u>Senkou span A</u>

For this we use the excel formula

$$= \frac{[\text{Tenkan Sen (conversion line) for 26 period} + \text{Kijun Sen (base line) for 26 period}]}{2}$$

Step 9:

We begin by calculating the <u>highest high for the 52 periods</u>.

For this, we use the excel formula

$$= \max(\text{High of period 1}:\text{high of period 52})$$

The data for a high of the respective period was respectively downloaded via Bloomberg L.P. for Education

Step 10:

We begin by calculating the Lowest low for the 52 periods.

For this, we use the excel formula

$$= \min(Low\ of\ period\ 1 : Low\ of\ period\ 52)$$

The data for low of the respective period was respectively downloaded via Bloomberg L.P. for Education

Step 11:

We will now calculate Senkou span B

For this, we use the excel formula

$$= \frac{(Highest\ High\ for\ the\ 52\ periods + Lowest\ Low\ for\ the\ 52\ periods)}{2}$$

Step-by-step Procedure for Bollinger Bands calculation:

Step 1:

We begin by calculating the Simple Moving Average for the 20 periods.

For this, we use the excel formula

$$= Average\ (close\ of\ period\ 1 : close\ of\ period\ 20)$$

Step 2:

We begin by calculating the Upper Bollinger Bands.

For this, we will assume ± 2 standard deviations (same as used by every Bollinger band)

For this, we use the excel formula

$$= SMA\ for\ 20\ Period\ of\ correspondiong\ period + [STDEVPA\ (close\ of\ period\ 1 : close\ of\ period\ 20) * 2]$$

Step 3:

We now calculate Lower Bollinger Bands

For this, we will assume ± 2 standard deviations (same as used by every Bollinger band)

For this, we use the excel formula

$$= SMA\ for\ 20\ Period\ of\ correspondiong\ period - [STDEVPA\ (close\ of\ period\ 1 : close\ of\ period\ 20) * 2]$$

Step-by-step Procedure for Stochastic Relative Strength Index calculation:

Step 1:

We begin by calculating the INPUT A for 14 periods.

For this, we use the excel formula

$$= close\ of\ the\ respective\ period - \min(Low\ of\ Period\ 1: Low\ of\ Period\ 14)$$

The data for a high of the respective period was respectively downloaded via Bloomberg L.P. for Education

Step 2:

We begin by calculating the INPUT B for 14 periods.

For this, we use the excel formula

$$= \max(High\ of\ Period\ 1: High\ of\ Period\ 14) - \min(Low\ of\ Period\ 1: Low\ of\ Period\ 14)$$

The data for low of the respective period was respectively downloaded via Bloomberg L.P. for Education

Step 3:

We now calculate %K

For this, we use the excel formula

$$= \left(\frac{INPUT\ A}{INPUT\ B}\right) * 100$$

Step 4:

We begin by calculating the Slow Stochastic.
For this, we use the excel formula

$$= \left\{\frac{Sum(Input\ A\ Period\ t: Input\ A\ Period\ t+3)}{Sum(Input\ B\ Period\ t: Input\ B\ Period\ t+3)}\right\} * 100$$

The data for a high of the respective period was respectively downloaded via Bloomberg L.P. for Education

Step 5:

We begin by calculating the Signal Line.
For this, we use the excel formula

$$= AVERAGE\ (Slow\ Stochastic\ Period\ t: Slow\ Stochastic\ Period\ t+3)$$

The data for low of the respective period was respectively downloaded via Bloomberg L.P. for Education
Once we have all the data collated, we will go ahead and use the above set of equations to calculate each micro-component of the indicators.
Once, we have done so we can now go ahead and begin financial modeling, we will use figure 2 and figure 3 based on which we pass through these micro components to omit to buy/sell and over bought and over sold indications. Once we have individual buy, sell overbought and oversold indications. It is now imperative to progress on to the second derivative of these buy, sell, overbought and oversold indications.
So, now since we are progressing, we will use logical functions in excel to map out possibilities and probabilities (including conditional probability).

We will define our logical function in a manner so that it takes into account the conditional probability to give us our perceived result.

Bullish Logical Functions

Hence, when we want our signal to omit to Buy and Oversold we have used the following Bullish logical functions

when we want our signal to omit to Buy and Oversold if Tenkan sen is greater than Kijun Sen given that Low is less than the lower Bollinger band, we have used this equation

=if(and(Tenkan Sen >Kijun Sen, Low < Lower Bollinger Band),"Buy and Oversold","")

when we want our signal to omit to Buy and Oversold if Tenkan sen is greater than Kijun Sen given that %K is less than 20, we have used this equation

=if(and(Tenkan Sen >Kijun Sen, %K <20),"Buy and Oversold","")

when we want our signal to omit to Buy and Oversold if Tenkan sen is greater than Kijun Sen given that the %K is greater than the Signal line, we have used this equation

=if(and(Tenkan Sen >Kijun Sen, %K > Signal Line),"Buy and Oversold","")

when we want our signal to omit to Buy and Oversold if Tenkan sen is greater than Kijun Sen given that the %K is greater than Signal line also given that %K is less 20, we have used this equation

=if(and(Tenkan Sen >Kijun Sen, %K > Signal Line, %K<20),"Buy and Oversold","")

Hence, when we want our signal to omit Buy and Oversold if Tenkan sen is greater than Kijun Sen given that the candle sticks are above the Kumo Clouds also given that the %K is greater than Signal line also given that %K is less 20, we have used this equation

=if(and(Tenkan Sen >Kijun Sen, low > Max(Senkou span A: Senkou Span B), %K > Signal Line, %K<20),"Buy and Oversold","")

When we want our signal to omit Buy and Oversold if Tenkan sen is greater than Kijun Sen given that the candle sticks are above the Kumo Clouds also given that the low is less than the lower Bollinger band, we have used this equation

=if(and(Tenkan Sen >Kijun Sen, low > Max(Senkou span A: Senkou Span B), Low < Lower Bollinger Band),"Buy and Oversold","")

When we want our signal to omit Buy and Oversold if Tenkan sen is greater than Kijun Sen given that the candle sticks are above the Kumo Clouds also given that the low is less than the lower Bollinger band also given that %K is less than 20, we have used this equation

=if(and(Tenkan Sen >Kijun Sen, low > Max(Senkou span A: Senkou Span B), Low < Lower Bollinger Band, %K <20),"Buy and Oversold","")

Lastly, when we want our signal to omit Buy and Oversold if Tenkan sen is greater than Kijun Sen given that the candle sticks are above the Kumo Clouds also given that the low is less than the lower Bollinger band also given that %K is greater than the signal line, we have used this equation

=if(and(Tenkan Sen >Kijun Sen, low > Max(Senkou span A: Senkou Span B), Low < Lower Bollinger Band, %K > SIgnal Line),"Buy and Oversold","")

Bearish Logical Functions

When we want our signal to omit Sell and Overbought signals we used the following bearish logical functions:

when we want our signal to omit Sell and overbought if Kijun sen is greater than Tenkan Sen given that Low is greater than the upper Bollinger band, we have used this equation

=if(and(Kijun Sen > Tenkan Sen, Low > Upper Bollinger Band),"Sell and Overbought","")

when we want our signal to omit Sell and overbought if Kijun sen is greater than Tenkan Sen given that %K is greater than 80, we have used this equation

=if(and(Kijun Sen > Tenkan Sen, %K>80),"Sell and Overbought","")

when we want our signal to omit Sell and overbought if Kijun sen is greater than Tenkan Sen given that %K is Lower than the Signal Line, we have used this equation

=if(and(Kijun Sen > Tenkan Sen, %K < Signal line),"Sell and Overbought","")

when we want our signal to omit Sell and overbought if Kijun sen is greater than Tenkan Sen given %K is greater than 80 also given that %K is Lower than the Signal Line, we have used this equation

=if(and(Kijun Sen > Tenkan Sen, %K > 80, %K < Signal line),"Sell and Overbought","")

when we want our signal to omit Sell and overbought if Kijun sen is greater than Tenkan Sen given candle sticks are below the Kumo cloud also given that %K is greater than 80 and also given that the %K is less than the Signal Line , we have used this equation

=if(and(Kijun Sen > Tenkan Sen, High < Min(Senkou span A: Senkou span B), %K > 80, %K < Signal line),"Sell and Overbought","")

when we want our signal to omit Sell and overbought if Kijun sen is greater than Tenkan Sen given candle sticks are below the Kumo cloud also given that high is greater than the upper bollinger bands, we have used this equation

=if(and(Kijun Sen > Tenkan Sen, High < Min(Senkou span A: Senkou span B), high > Upper Bollinger Band),"Sell and Overbought","")

when we want our signal to omit Sell and overbought if Kijun sen is greater than Tenkan Sen given candle sticks are below the Kumo cloud also given that high is greater than the upper Bollinger bands, also given that %K is greater than 80 we have used this equation

=if(and(Kijun Sen > Tenkan Sen, High < Min(Senkou span A: Senkou span B), high > Upper Bollinger Band, %K >80),"Sell and Overbought","")

when we want our signal to omit Sell and overbought if Kijun sen is greater than Tenkan Sen given candle sticks are below the Kumo cloud also given that high is greater than the upper Bollinger bands, also given that %K is less than Signal line we have used this equation

=if(and(Kijun Sen > Tenkan Sen, High < Min(Senkou span A: Senkou span B), high > Upper Bollinger Band, %K < Signal Line),"Sell and Overbought","")

These Bullish and bearish indicator omittances are used as a trading guidance and they form the bedrock for fixed length trading strategy as well as Sharma Amalgamation strategy.

Once we have these then the third derivative is formed namely "Fixed Length trading strategy" and "Sharma Amalgamation"

Fixed Length Trading Strategy

The fixed length trading strategy will also be modelling using logical functions in excel.

The Formula we will use for fixed length trading strategy is as follows:

=If(or(Signal 1 = "Buy and oversold", Signal 2 = "Buy and oversold", Signal 3 = "Buy and oversold", Signal 4 = "Buy and oversold", Signal 5 = "Buy and oversold", Signal 6 = "Buy and oversold", Signal 7 = "Buy and oversold", Signal 8 = "Buy and oversold"),(Ln(P_e/P_b)*100))

Where P_e and P_b are Period ending (10th day) and Period Beginning (1st Day)

Sharma Amalgamation

The Sharma Amalgamation trading strategy will partly also be modelling using logical functions in excel.

For the first part we must process this manually,

Steps
Step 1: Note the first "buy and oversold" signal period (across all 8 bullish signals)
Step 2: Then ignore all other buy signals
Step 3: Secondly, Note the next "sell and overbought" signal period (across all 8 bearish signals)
Step 4: Once again, ignore all the rest of the sell signals,
Step 5: Then, repeat step 1 for entire number of observations.

However, this can become manually stimulating for big data such as for this research for S&P 500, FTSE 100, Nifty 50 and S&P/TSX 60. Where we had to perform this for 28000 observations manually
Then we use the logical test Formula for Sharma Amalgamation trading strategy is as follows:

$$=Ln(P_e/P_b)*100$$

Where P_e and P_b are Period ending (Variable period calculated manually) and Period Beginning (Variable period calculated manually)

Technical Indicator Signal List:

It can be noticed that the we have various signals omitted by the Sharma amalgamation stock screening mechanism of Ichimoku Kinko Hyo, Bollinger Bands and Stochastic Relative Strength Index.

The bullish signals belong to three broad category's which are shown in Figure 2 as Weak, Mezzanine and Strong and the underlying opportunity is explained using aa visual aid as shown in Venn diagram 1

Strength	BUY	Buy/Sell or Overbought/Oversold
Weak	If Tenkan Sen > Kijun Sen	Buy
	Low > Max (Senkou Span A: Senkou Span B)	buy
	If Low < Lower Bollinger Band	Oversold
	If %K < 20	Oversold
	If %K > Signal Line	Oversold
Mezzanine	If Tenkan Sen > Kijun Sen and Low < Lower Bollinger Band	Buy and Oversold
	If Tenkan Sen > Kijun Sen and %K < 20	Buy and Oversold
	If Tenkan Sen > Kijun Sen and %K > Signal Line	Buy and Oversold
	If Tenkan Sen > Kijun Sen and Low > Max (Senkou Span A: Senkou Span B)	Buy
Strong	If Tenkan Sen > Kijun Sen and %K > Signal Line and %K < 20	Buy and Oversold
	If Tenkan Sen > Kijun Sen and Low > Max (Senkou Span A: Senkou Span B) and %K > Signal Line and %K < 20	Buy and Oversold
	If Tenkan Sen > Kijun Sen and Low > Max (Senkou Span A: Senkou Span B) and low < Lower Bollinger band	Buy and Oversold
	If Tenkan Sen > Kijun Sen and Low > Max (Senkou Span A: Senkou Span B) and low < Lower Bollinger band and %K <20	Buy and Oversold
	If Tenkan Sen > Kijun Sen and Low > Max (Senkou Span A: Senkou Span B) and low < Lower Bollinger band and %K > Signal line	Buy and Oversold

Figure 2: A table illustrating buy and Oversold signals as emitted by Sharma amalgamation stock screening mechanism.
Venn Diagram 2: A Venn diagram indicating "Sell and oversold"

The bearish signals also belong to three broad categories which are shown in Figure 3 as Weak, Mezzanine and Strong and the underlying opportunity is explained using aa visual aid as shown in Venn diagram 2. These signals

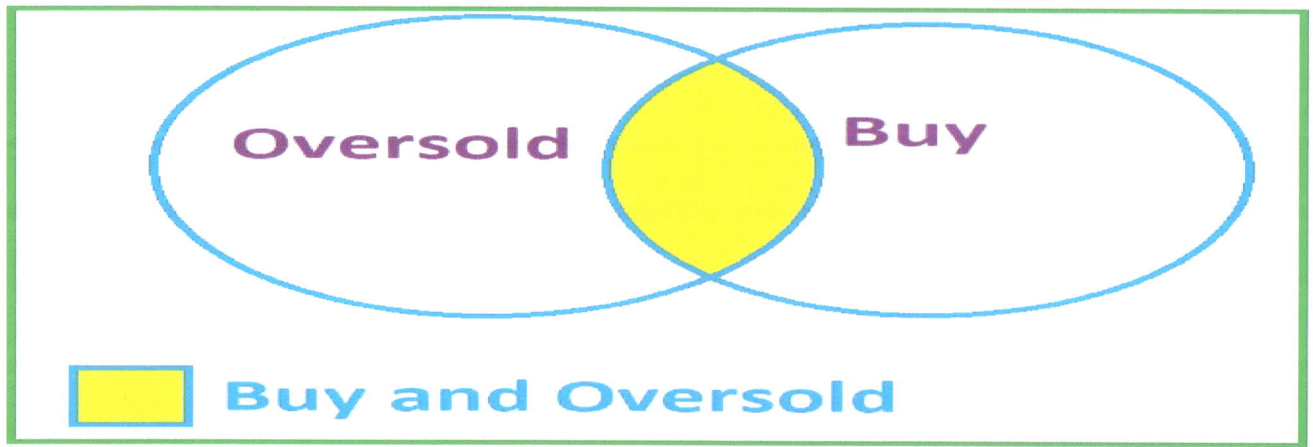

Strength	SELL	Buy/Sell or Overbought/Oversold
Weak	If Tenkan Sen < Kijun Sen	Sell
	High < Min (Senkou Span A: Senkou Span B)	sell
	If High > Upper Bollinger Band	Overbought
	If %K > 80	Overbought
	If %K < Signal Line	Overbought
Mezzanine	If Kijun sen > Tenkan Sen and Low > Upper Bollinger Band	Sell and Overbought
	If Kijun sen > Tenkan Sen and %K > 80	Sell and Overbought
	if Kijun Sen > Tenkan Sen and %K < Signal Line	Sell and Overbought
	If Tenkan Sen< Kijun Sen and High < Min (Senkou Span A: Senkou Span B)	Sell
Strong	If Tenkan Sen < Kijun Sen and %K < Signal Line and %K > 80	Sell and Overbought
	If Tenkan Sen < Kijun Sen and High < Min (Senkou Span A: Senkou Span B) and %K < Signal Line and %K > 80	Sell and Overbought
	If Tenkan Sen < Kijun Sen and High < Min (Senkou Span A: Senkou Span B) and If High > Upper Bollinger Band	Sell and Overbought
	If Tenkan Sen < Kijun Sen and High < Min (Senkou Span A: Senkou Span B) and If High > Upper Bollinger Band and %K >80	Sell and Overbought
	If Tenkan Sen < Kijun Sen and High < Min (Senkou Span A: Senkou Span B) and If High > Upper Bollinger Band and %K < Signal line	Sell and Overbought

Figure 3: A table illustrating sell and Overbought signals as emitted by Sharma amalgamation stock screening mechanism.
Venn Diagram 2: A Venn diagram indicating "Sell and oversold"

Thus, essentially it is inferred from this notion that "Buy and oversold" and "Sell and Overbought" are essentially conditional probability as shown in Venn Diagram 1 and Venn Diagram 2. This concludes that "Buy and oversold" is second derivate of "Buy" and "Oversold". On the other hand, conclusion can be made that "Sell and Overbought" is the second derivative of "Sell" and "Overbought".

The oversold and overbought indications are essential a mechanism of timing the entry and exit from positions, where as Buy and sell indications are a mechanism for testing overall market trend. Thus, an amalgamation

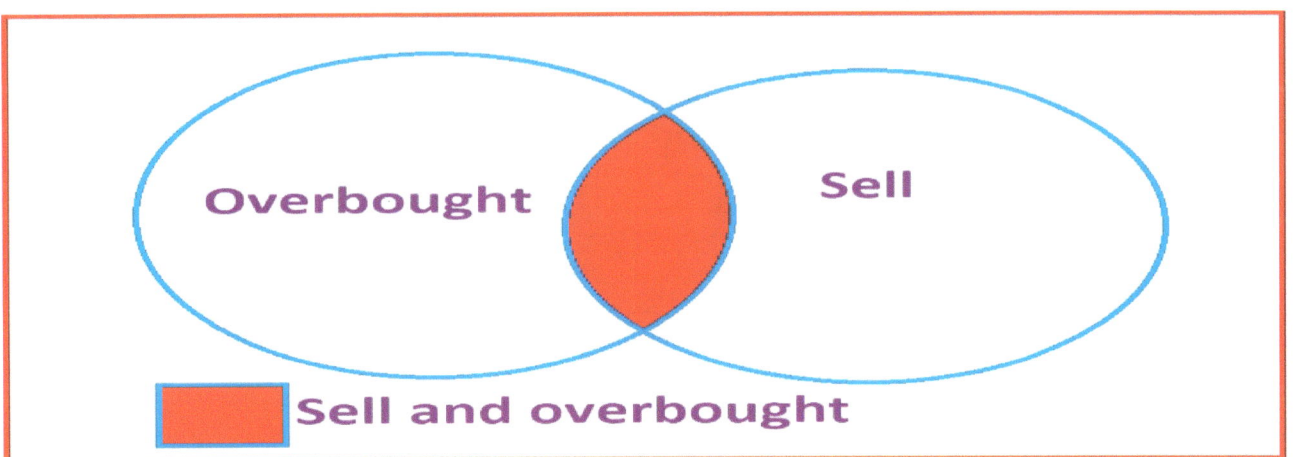

1. DESCRIPTIVE STATISTICS

	Buy and hold strategy returns			
	S&P 500	**FTSE 100**	**Nifty 50**	**S&P/TSX**
Total Return	2014.857	1163.929	3613.535	1353.266
Number of signals	7100	7159	6748	7083
mean return	0.283783	0.162583	0.535497	0.191058
skewness	-0.992616	-0.718765	-0.125939	-1.118851
kurtosis	6.684306	3.683301	3.196097	6.584992
Number of winning trades	3904	3743	3841	3845
number of losing trades	2791	2952	2906	2843
Percentage of winning trades	58.31217	55.90739	56.92901	57.49103
Variance	9.487038	9.865029	29.80361	9.307806

Table 1: A table indicating buy and hold strategy returns

Table 1 shows, the returns for buy and hold strategy for S&P 500, FTSE 100, Nifty 50 and S&P/TSX. It can be inferred that mean return for the 30-year period can be seen outperforming in Nifty 50 as compared to its peers. It can also be noted the Nifty 50 has omitted the least number of signals during this 30-year period.

Nifty 50 has the most positively skewed distribution whereas, S&P/TSX has the most negatively skewed distribution. Another, metric of distribution is the kurtosis and inference can be drawn from Table 1 that all the distributions for S&P 500, FTSE 100, Nifty 50 and S&P/TSX are leptokurtic. Ipso facto, Nifty 50 is the least leptokurtic as opposed to S&P500 which is the most leptokurtic at a staggering kurtosis of 6.684306

	Fixed length (10 days) strategy based on technical analysis technique returns			
	S&P 500	**FTSE 100**	**Nifty 50**	**S&P/TSX**
Total Return	345.796022	-191.007294	1315.514	570.7262
Number of signals	57489	50716	54064	57400
mean return	0.14695964	-0.08938105	0.624651	0.252534
skewness	-0.72239108	-0.53279643	-0.3129	-0.62749
kurtosis	2.39644728	1.19880783	4.457965	1.871908
Number of winning trades	2384	2723	2334	2468
number of losing trades	1313	1526	1553	440
Percentage of winning trades	64.4847173	64.0856672	60.04631	84.86933
Variance	6.33993673	7.00258026	28.48603	6.359332

Table 2: A table indicating Fixed length strategy based on technical amalgamation returns

Table 2 shows, the returns for Fixed length strategy based on technical analysis for S&P 500, FTSE 100, Nifty 50 and S&P/TSX. It can be inferred that mean return for the 30-year period can once again be seen outperforming in Nifty

50 as compared to its peers. It can also be noted the FTSE 100 has de-throned nifty 50 by omitting the least number of signals during this 30-year period.

Once again, Nifty 50 has the most positively skewed distribution whereas, S&P 500 has ousted S&P/TSX to become the most negatively skewed distribution. Another, metric of distribution is the kurtosis and inference can be drawn from Table 2 that the distributions for S&P 500, FTSE 100, and S&P/TSX are platykurtic whereas Nifty 50 is in an elite club of its own due its leptokurtic kurtosis tendency. Ipso facto, Nifty 50 is the only leptokurtic as opposed to FTSE 100 which is the most platykurtic at a mundane kurtosis of 1.19880783.

	Time varying conditional strategy ("Sharma Amalgamation") return			
	S&P 500	**FTSE 100**	**Nifty 50**	**S&P/TSX**
Total Return	65.61376	62.6812	336.4831	136.7575
Number of signals	140	138	240	123
mean return	0.46867	0.454212	2.804026	1.11185
skewness	1.071886	1.113168	2.383503	1.408148
kurtosis	2.644128	2.234812	8.317393	4.498597
Number of winning trades	67	62	54	58
number of losing trades	73	76	66	65
Percentage of winning trades	47.85714	44.92754	45	47.15447
Variance	25.30129	18.46134	127.9088	30.33766

Table 3: A table Time varying conditional strategy ("Sharma Amalgamation") returns

Table 3 shows, the returns for Time varying conditional strategy (Sharma Amalgamation) for S&P 500, FTSE 100, Nifty 50 and S&P/TSX. It can be inferred that mean return for the 30-year period can once again be seen outperforming in Nifty 50 as compared to its peers. It can also be noted the S&P/TSX has de-throned FTSE 100 by omitting the least number of signals during this 30-year period, whereas Nifty 50 omitted a staggering 240 signals.

Astonishingly, all S&P 500, FTSE 100, Nifty 50 and S&P/TSX are positively skewed. However, again, Nifty 50 has the most positively skewed distribution at an impressive 2.383503, whereas, S&P 500 retains its position to remain the least positively skewed distribution. Another, metric of distribution is the kurtosis and material change can be noticed from Table 3 that the distributions for S&P 500, FTSE 100, and S&P/TSX and Nifty 50 are all leptokurtic. Nifty 50 Has been joined in its elite club of leptokurtic kurtosis tendency. Ipso facto, Nifty 50 is at aa remarkable kurtosis of 8.317393 as opposed to FTSE 100 which is the least leptokurtic at a disappointing kurtosis of 2.234812.

It can also be inferred from Table 3, Table 2, and Table 1 that the mean returns in "Sharma Amalgamation" vastly outperform the mean returns in buy and hold strategy, as well as Fixed length strategy based on technical analysis. The winning trades in fixed length strategy vastly outnumber the winning trades in Sharma amalgamation. Percentage of winning trades is also higher in fixed length strategy based on technical analysis.

2. DATA ANALYSIS

Data Analysis is a resilient complexity which must be tackled head on with constructive and conclusive actions.

The equation for the T-test is defined as the following by Brock et. Al (1992):

$$\text{t-statistics for buy (Buy and over sold)} = \frac{\mu_r - \mu_n}{\sqrt{\frac{\sigma^2}{N} + \frac{\sigma^2}{N_r}}}$$

Equation 1: Equation to compare buy (buy and oversold) signals against the 10 day buy and hold strategy

Where μ_r and N_r are the average return and the number of buy (or buy and oversold) signals, μ_n and μ_n are the mean and number of trades from the buy and hold strategy (or Sharma amalgamation strategy), and σ^2 is the variance

For the T-test (equation 1), the following hypothesis will be used

$H_0: \mu_r = \mu_n$ (The two samples are alike at a 5% significance level)

$H_0: \mu_r \neq \mu_n$ (The two samples are different at a 5% significance level)

Equation 2: Null and alternative hypothesis for comparing Sharma amalgamation returns against Fixed length strategy return and Sharma amalgamation returns against Buy and hold strategy returns.

Thus, it is imperative to compare the critical value to the calculated value to be able to decipher whether to reject the null hypothesis. If the calculated value lies outside of the positive and negative critical values, then we can reject the null hypothesis.

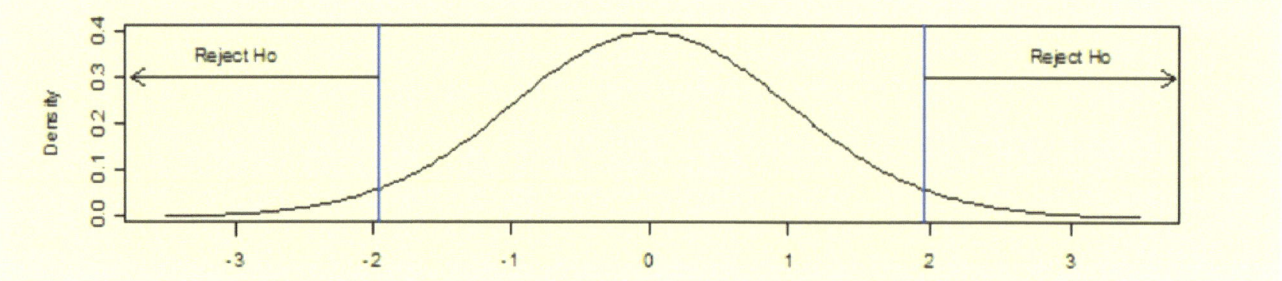

Figure 4: A diagram depicting the Two tailed test rejection regions

We can see infer from figure 4 that if the calculated value is inside the positive and negative critical values, then we fail to reject the null hypothesis

Buy and hold vs Time varying conditional strategy return ("Sharma Amalgamation")				
	S&P 500	FTSE 100	Nifty 50	S&P/TSX
Calculated Value	0.433310886	0.793256	3.094621	1.849136
Critical Value	± 1.97705	± 1.9773	± 1.9699	± 1.97944

Table 4: A table indicating buy and hold strategy returns

Inference can be made from table 4 between the Time varying conditional strategy ("Sharma Amalgamation") against a buy and hold strategy.

Thus, firstly, in the case of S&P 500 the critical value (-1.97705) < calculated value (0.433310886) < the critical value (1.97705)

    Thus, in the case of S&P 500 as calculated lies between the negative and the positive critical value, ipso facto, we fail to reject the null hypothesis

Secondly, in the case of FTSE 100 the critical value (-1.9773) < calculated value (0.793256) < the critical value (1.9773)

    Thus, in the case of FTSE 100 as calculated lies between the negative and the positive critical value, ipso facto, we fail to reject the null hypothesis

Thirdly, in the case of Nifty 50 the calculated value (3.094621) > the critical value (± 1.9699)

    Thus, in the case of Nifty 50 as calculated lies outside the critical value, ipso facto, we reject the null hypothesis

Finally, in the case of S&P/TSX the critical value (-1.97944) < calculated value (1.849136) < the critical value (1.977944)

    Thus, in the case of S&P/TSX as calculated lies between the negative and the positive critical value, ipso facto, we fail to reject the null hypothesis

Fixed length strategy vs Time varying conditional strategy return ("Sharma Amalgamation")				
	S&P 500	FTSE 100	Nifty 50	S&P/TSX
Calculated Value	0.7565277	1.485448	2.983821	1.729883
Critical Value	± 1.97705	± 1.9773	± 1.9699	± 1.97944

Table 5: A table indicating buy and hold strategy returns

Inference can be made from table 5 between the Time-varying conditional strategy ("Sharma Amalgamation") against Fixed length strategy.

Thus, firstly, in the case of S&P 500 the critical value (-1.97705) < calculated value (0.7565277) < the critical value (1.97705)

    Thus, in the case of S&P 500 as calculated lies between the negative and the positive critical value, ipso facto, we fail to reject the null hypothesis

Secondly, in the case of FTSE 100 the critical value (-1.9773) < the calculated value (1.485448) < the critical value (1.9773)

    Thus, in the case of S&P 500 as calculated lies between the negative and the positive critical value, ipso facto, we fail to reject the null hypothesis

Thirdly, in the case of Nifty 50 the calculated value (2.983821) > the critical value (± 1.9699)

    Thus, in the case of Nifty 50 as calculated lies outside the critical value, ipso facto, we reject the null hypothesis

Finally, in the case of S&P/TSX the critical value (-1.97944) < the calculated value (1.729883) < the critical value (1.97944)

    Thus, in the case of S&P/TSX as calculated lies between the negative and the positive critical value, ipso facto, we fail to reject the null hypothesis

3. DATA INTERPRETATION

Empirical evidence draws some stark conclusion, if we compare table 1, table 2 and table 3, we evidence that the frequency of winning trades outnumbers the frequency losing trades in Sharma amalgamation.

However, do not discredit Sharma amalgamation, as this is a mere concealment.

> *Inverted loss aversion: This is an inherent underlying of the "Sharma amalgamation" and this is the converse of loss aversion where we let the in the money(winning) positions continue and immediately terminate any loss making or potentially loss turning positions.*

The solemn realisation draws conclusion from that Sharma Amalgamations outperform both the buy and hold strategy as well as the fixed length strategy. This is the reason which reinforces our belief that Sharma Amalgamations is a superior trading strategy as compared to Buy and hold as well as Fixed Length Trading strategy. This becomes evident from a staggering mean return using Sharma Amalgamations which stand based on our empirical evidence of 280.4026% in Nifty 50, 111.185% mean return in S&P/TSX, 46.867% mean returns in S&P 500 and 45.4212% mean return in FTSE 100.

Thus, pursuant to research ideology of inverted loss aversion by Sharma amalgamation, the technique dictates the liquidation of positions at the first "sell and overbought" signal emission. It is thus the anticipation of the research that by abiding by the swing trading technique the losses are mitigated while profits are explosive.

Sharma amalgamation has empirically proven that these inherent behavioural science techniques are true in its nature.

Sharma amalgamation has a higher percentage of losing trade, however, Sharma amalgamation is more efficient in nipping the loss-making trades in its buds, whilst taking a hands-off approach of fostering the winning trades to thrive. Thereby, when Sharma amalgamations has losses these losses (out-of-the-money positions) are mitigated, on the other hand, when Sharma amalgamations has profits (in-the-money positions) it deploys a hands-off approach and allows the positions to flourish.

By immediately eliminating losing trades Sharma Amalgamation has been able create a trading strategy which cap the downside while benefitting from the upside potential. This enhances the use ability of Sharma Amalgamations of Ichimoku Kinko Hyo, Bollinger Bands and Stochastic RSI by industry and the study of this cluster by academicians.

1. Efficient Market Hypothesis and its impact on technical Analysis

	Efficient Market Hypothesis		
Item	**Strong form efficient market**	**Semi strong form efficient market**	**Weak form efficient market**
Definition	Prices reflect all past prices and volume data	Prices reflect all past price and volume data and all public information	Prices reflect all past price and volume data and all public and non-public information
Implication	Charts/Technical trading will not lead to excess returns	Charts/technical trading and fundamental analysis will not lead to excess returns	No excess returns are possible
Significance	Fundamental analysis can lead to alpha	Insider information can lead to alpha	No alpha possible

Table 6: Indicating Efficient Market Hypothesis and its impact on Technical analysis

Table 6 shows the efficient market hypothesis, it consists of (1) Strong form efficient market (2) semi strong form efficient market and (3) Weak form

Empirical evidence from Sharma Amalgamation states that S&P 500, FTSE 100, Nifty 50 and S&P/TSX 60 cannot be weak form efficient market as we are generating alpha. On the other hand, S&P 500, FTSE 100, Nifty 50 and S&P/TSX 60 can not be Strong form efficient market as we have empirical evidence that we can make excess returns using technical analysis. Lastly, Efficient Market Hypothesis for S&P 500, FTSE 100, Nifty 50 and S&P/TSX 60 in the case of semi strong form efficient market states that neither fundamental nor technical analysis can be used to create excess profits.

However, as empirical evidence suggests we can indeed make excess returns using technical analysis. Hence, considering our empirical findings the Efficient Market Hypothesis (EMH) is incoherent branded redundant as an effective guidance mechanism for creating profit in terms of technical analysis.

2. Recommendations

A Masters dissertation for MSc. Investment Management does not do justice to the topic at hand. This is such an intrinsic and complex topic that this is not even the tip of the iceberg. For the finance community to draw empirical conviction on this effectiveness of this method a Ph.D. level research is warranted.

In the beginning of this dissertation certain questions were set to be answered. We can decipher the inference from Sharma Amalgamations to these questions are as follows:

1. We can trade based on buy/sell signals, oversold/overbought signals, permutations and combinations generated by technical analysis to create alpha in United Kingdom using FTSE 100
2. We can trade based on buy/sell signals, oversold/overbought signals, permutations and combinations generated by technical analysis to create alpha in United States of America using S&P 500
3. We can trade based on buy/sell signals, oversold/overbought signals, permutations and combinations generated by technical analysis to create alpha in Republic of India using Nifty 50
4. We can trade based on buy/sell signals, oversold/overbought signals, permutations and combinations generated by technical analysis to create alpha in Canada using S&P/TSX 60.

Sharma Amalgamation should be used as a technical analysis cluster tool by professional traders and academicians to enhance their profitability and to foster a wider array of confirmation of signal using the "Buy and oversold" cluster or "Sell and overbought" cluster.

Using these clusters can help traders predict stock price movements and enhance their return on Investments. Sharma Amalgamation should be taught to traders in Big 4 investment Banks and trading houses. Buy and Sell side trading executives can use these techniques to considerably enhance the mean returns of their trading desk profitability.

It is imperative that the next stage of process naturally is developing Sharma amalgamations into an algorithm to test on real time share prices in a demo version which eventually is intended to be using by various financial institutions.

Sharma Amalgamations should also be tested in various setting Emerging Markets vs Frontier Markets, developed markets vs frontier markets and Emerging Markets vs Developed markets. It can also be niched down to each stock or by asset class. Since Ichimoku Kinko Hyo is not timeframe constrained we can also alter the time patterns to better enhance the usability of Sharma Amalgamations

Sharma Amalgamation can be enhanced with the usage of Artificial Intelligence and Machine Learning. Using Sharma Amalgamation to map an algorithm various institution can automate their market trading activity.

There is also, further scope to enhance and polish Sharma Amalgamation fundamentally by introducing complementing technical analysis techniques such as the Elliot Wave Theory or the Fibonacci Retracement to make the analysis more efficient.

Appendices

Calculated Value based on fixed length strategy vs buy and hold strategy				
	S&P 500	FTSE 100	Nifty 50	S&P/TSX
Average return for fixed length signal (U_r)	0.14696	-0.089381	0.624651	0.252534
Average return for buy and hold strategy (U)	0.283783	0.162583	0.535497	0.191058
variance from fixed length signal	6.339937	7.00258	28.48603	6.359332
Variance from buy and hold strategy	9.487038	9.865029	29.80361	9.307806
Number of observations for Fixed length signal (N_r)	57489	50716	54064	57400
Number of observations for buy and hold strategy (N)	7100	7159	6748	7083
second half of denominator	0.00011	0.000138	0.000527	0.000111
first half of denominator	0.001336	0.001378	0.004417	0.001314
Calculated Value	-3.597513	-6.471115	1.267997	1.628584

Table X: Table indicating the calculation of calculated value for Fixed length strategy vs buy and hold strategy

Calculated value based on fixed length strategy vs Time varying conditional strategy return ("Sharma Amalgamation")				
	S&P 500	FTSE 100	Nifty 50	S&P/TSX
Average return for Sharma Amalgamation (U_r)	0.4686697	0.45421161	2.804026	1.11185
Average return for Fixed length strategy (U)	0.14695964	-0.08938105	0.624651	0.252534
variance from Sharma Amalgamation	25.3012937	18.4613409	127.9088	30.33766
Variance from Fixed length strategy	6.33993673	7.00258026	28.48603	6.359332
Number of observations for Sharma Amalgamation (N_r)	140	138	240	123
Number of observations for Fixed length strategy (N)	57489	50716	54064	57400
second half of denominator	0.18072353	0.13377783	0.532953	0.246648
First half of denominator	0.00011028	0.00013807	0.000527	0.000111
Calculated Value	0.7565277	1.48544815	2.983821	1.729883

Table Y: Table indicating the calculation of calculated value for Fixed length strategy vs buy and hold strategy

Calculated Value based on buy and hold vs Time varying conditional strategy return ("Sharma Amalgamation")				
	S&P 500	FTSE 100	Nifty 50	S&P/TSX
Average return for Sharma Amalgamation (Ur)	0.46867	0.454212	2.804026	1.11185
Average return for buy and hold strategy (U)	0.283783	0.162583	0.535497	0.191058
variance from Sharma Amalgamation	25.30129	18.46134	127.9088	30.33766
Variance from Buy and hold strategy	9.487038	9.865029	29.80361	9.307806
Number of observations for Sharma Amalgamation (Nr)	140	138	240	123
Number of observations for buy and hold strategy (N)	7100	7159	6748	7083
second half of denominator	0.180724	0.133778	0.532953	0.246648
first half of denominator	0.001336	0.001378	0.004417	0.001314
Calculated Value	0.433311	0.793256	3.094621	1.849136

Table Z: Table indicating the calculation of calculated value for Fixed length strategy vs buy and hold strategy

Signal Integration sheet

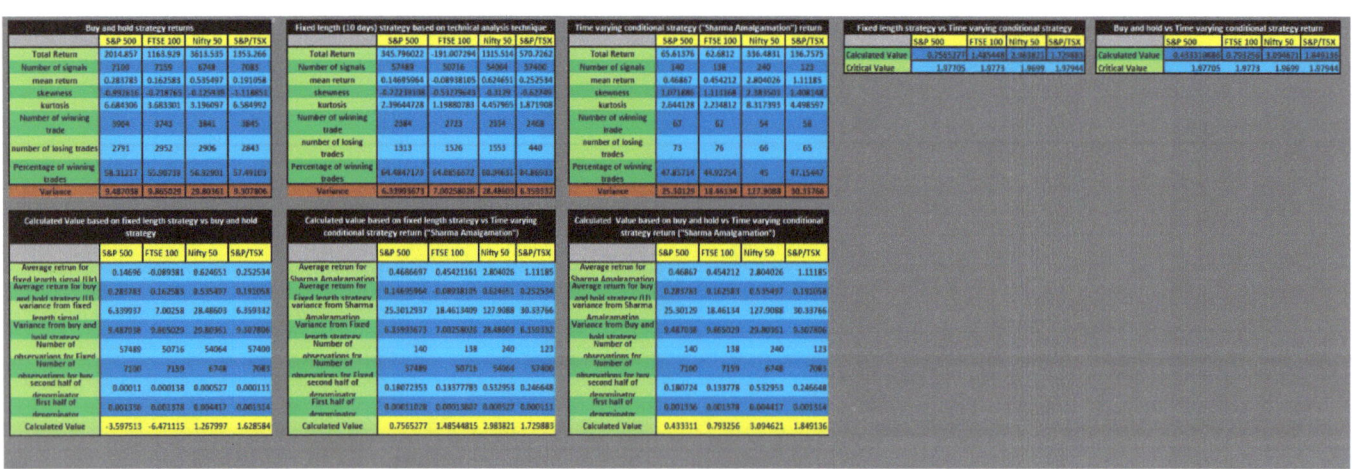

References

1. Brock, W., Lakonishok, J., and LeBaron, B. (1992) *'Simple Technical Trading Rules and the stochastic Properties of Stock Returns'*. Journal of Finance 47(5),1731-1764
2. Eirini, M., (2007) 'Portfolio creation and stocks evaluation with chaos theory' Unpublished Dissertation. Greenwich: Greenwich Business school - University of Greenwich
3. Fang, J., Jacobsen, B., Qin, Y., (2012)'Predictability of the Simple Technical Trading Rules: An Out-of-Sample Test'. Unpublished Phd Thesis. Edinburgh: The University of Edinburgh
4. Fang, J., (2014) 'Essays on Technical Analysis on Stock Markets' Unpublished Phd Thesis. Albany, New Zealand: The Massey University, New Zealand
5. Investopedia (N.d.) 'Bollinger Bands'[Online] available from <https://www.investopedia.com/terms/b/bollingerbands.asp>[2 August 2018]
6. Investopedia (N.d.) 'Ichimoku Kinko HYo'[Online] available from <https://www.investopedia.com/terms/i/ichimokuchart.asp>[7 August 2018]
7. Investopedia (N.d.) 'StochRSI'[Online] available from <https://www.investopedia.com/terms/s/stochrsi.asp>[6 August 2018]
8. Kuepper, J., (N.d.) *Technical Analysis: Indicators And Oscillators* [Online] available from <https://www.investopedia.com/university/technical/techanalysis10.asp>[31 July 2018]
9. Kumar, R., (2017) 'Technical and Fundamental Anlyses of Sensex Representative companies' Unpublished PhD Thesis. Rohtak, India: Department of Commerce - Maharshi dayanand University, Rohtak
10. Larsen, F., (2007) 'Automatic stock market trading based on Technical Analysis' Unpublished Dissertation. Norway: Department of Computer and Information Science - Norwegian University of Science and Technology
11. Malkiel, B., (1981) 'A Random walk down wall street' Norton (2)
12. Manic, V., (2017) 'Investment based on Technical Analysis' Unpublished Dissertation. Brno, Czech Republic: Faculty of Economica and Administration - Masaryk University
13. Mashaushi, K., (2006) 'An analysis of technical trading strategies' Unpublished Phd Thesis. Leeds: Leeds Business School - The University of leeds
14. Muller, D., (2013) 'Ichimoku for Dummies: "Shattering the cloud"'[Online] available from <https://www.aktieguiden.com/Message/Attachment/1159527>[17 July 2018]
15. Rechethin, M., (2014) 'Machine-learning classification techniques for the analysis and prediction of high-frequency stock direction'Unpublished Phd Thesis. Iowa: University of Iowa
16. Venkataramani, C., (2003)'Random Walk HYpothesis and profitability of Momentum based trading rules': Unpublished Phd Thesis. Pennsylvania: Wharton School of Business - The University of Pennsylvania